MW01269189

TUCKER
CARLSON

Table of Contents

Chapter 1

Early Life

On May 16, 1969, Tucker McNear Carlson was born in the Mission District of San Francisco, California. The oldest son of San Franciscan artist Lisa McNear and US ambassador to the Seychelles, Dick Carlson, who was also the director of Voice of America and president of the Corporation for Public Broadcasting. Tucker was followed almost two years later by a younger brother, Buckley.

In 1976, when Carlson was six, his parents divorced. Dick Carlson had had a difficult start in life, having been placed in the Home for Little Wanderers orphanage by his birth parents, teenagers Richard Boynton and Dorothy Anderson, who had not been able to provide for their son. He was subsequently adopted when he was two by the people who raised him, Carl and Mainer Florence Carlson.

After the divorce, Dick Carlson applied for and got custody of the two Tucker boys, while Lisa left her sons to pursue a bohemian lifestyle in Paris. According to the New Yorker, Carlson's attitude towards his mother was that it was a "Totally bizarre situation — which I never talk about, because it was actually not really part of my life at all."

When Carlson was in first grade, he moved with his father and brother to the La Jolla neighborhood of San Diego, California, where he attended La Jolla Country Day School. A wealthy man, Dick Carlson owned properties in Nevada, Vermont, Maine, and Nova Scotia. The family lived in a house overlooking the La Jolla Beach and Tennis Club.

In 1979, Dick Carlson remarried. His new wife, Patricia Caroline Swanson, had also been married before. She was the daughter of Gilbert Carl Swanson and niece of Senator J William Fulbright. She was an heiress to Swanson Enterprises, although, by the time of her marriage to Dick Carlson, the Swansons had sold the brand to the Campbell Soup Company.

The Carlsons briefly enrolled Tucker at the Collège du Léman, a Swiss boarding school. However, Carlson later revealed that he had been 'kicked out.' So instead, he went to St George's School, another boarding school, in Middletown, Rhode Island. This is where he met and started dating the headmaster's daughter, Susan Andrews, whom he would later marry and go on to have four children with. His classmates would describe him as "a self-assured conservative who wasn't afraid to speak his mind."

After leaving school, Carlson went to Trinity College in Hartford, Connecticut, where he graduated with a BA in history in 1991. That same year, Carlson married Andrews in the chapel at their old high school. His college yearbook states that he was a member of the so-called 'Dan White Society.' Dan White was the political assassin who killed George Moscone, the mayor of San Francisco Mayor, and Harvey Milk, a member of the San Francisco Board of Supervisors. However, little is known about what this society was about, nor Carlson's role within it.

Following graduation, Carlson applied to join the Central Intelligence Agency, but his application was unsuccessful. So instead, his father suggested that he pursue a career in journalism.

Chapter 2

Early Career

Carlson's journalism career began working as a fact-checker for *Policy Review,* a national conservative journal. Carlson later said, "I ended up working for this magazine because the standards are so low." His former editor, Adam Myerson, said that "Tucker was an enterprising, hard-working, shoe-leather reporter."

He then made the jump into journalism proper when he started work as a reporter at the *Arkansas Democrat Gazette,* a newspaper based in Little Rock, Arkansas. His then-editor, Paul Greenberg, said of Carlson that "Tucker was a pleasure to work with. I knew he would fit right in in Arkansas when I discovered that he chewed tobacco."

Carlson actively pursued a position with *The Weekly Standard* news magazine, which he joined in 1995. He said that once he heard of the magazine's founding, he was worried that he would be "written off as a wing nut" if he had moved to *The American Spectator* instead.

Carlson wrote for various publications over the years, including *Talk* magazine. Tina Brown, who worked with him there, said that "Tucker is a tremendously good writer, and I always thought it was a real shame that he kind of like got sucked into this TV mania thing." One of the pieces Carlson produced was a 1999 interview with then-Governor George W. Bush. In the article, Carlson quoted Bush mocking Karla Faye Tucker, who was executed in 1998 for killing two people with a pickaxe during a burglary. The first woman to be executed in the United States for more than a decade, her gender and conversion to Christianity had prompted a call for her sentence to be commuted to life without parole. Later in the article, Carlson reported that Bush repeatedly swore, using the F-word. His article caused bad publicity for Bush's 2000 presidential campaign. In response, Bush stated that "Mr. Carlson misread, mischaracterized me. He's a good reporter. He just misunderstood about how serious that was. I take the death penalty very seriously." However, the piece attracted praise from liberals like Democratic consultant Bob Shrum, who described it as "vivid." Later, Carlson himself said that "I thought I'd be ragged for writing a puffy piece. My wife said people are going to think you're hunting for a job in the Bush campaign."

Over the years of his print journalism career, Carlson worked for numerous publications, including *New York* magazine, *Reader's Digest, Esquire, Slate, The Weekly Standard, The New Republic, The New York Times Magazine, The Daily Beast,* and *The Wall Street Journal.* John F Harris of *Politico* later observed that Carlson was "viewed ... as an important voice of the intelligentsia" during his time as a print journalist.

In 2001, Carlson and his father went to the Afghanistan-Pakistan border to research material for a piece on the Taliban for *New York.* As they were flying to Dubai, their plane crashed on the runway. In an email, Dick Carlson wrote that "There was some kind of serious problem with the landing gear as we came in over the Arabian Sea – it felt as if we hit something in the air, though I can't imagine what it could have been… Tucker and I were in the very front. The wheels seemed to collapse and the right wing hit the runway at a couple hundred miles an hour. Flames and huge billows of smoke shot up along the windows and an engine on the right wing fell off, then that wing itself collapsed as we spun sideways... We skidded off into sand... which probably saved us from a fatal fire... It was Tucker who threw open the exit door by the cockpit. I've always wondered what it was like to go down those chutes. It was pretty great, actually, on a couple of levels... Firetrucks arrived pretty fast, so much that many of the latter passengers sliding down the chutes were soaked with foam."

Miraculously, both father and son walked away unscathed from the potentially fatal crash.

In 2000, Carlson made the jump to television when he co-hosted the short-lived CNN show *The Spin Room.* On this show and up until 2006, Carlson sported his signature bow ties, an affectation he had acquired in boarding school. Following this appearance, Carlson won the co-host spot on *Crossfire,* in which he alternated with Robert Novak to present right-wing opinions while James Carville and Paul Begala alternated as left-wing co-hosts.

In October 2004, Carlson was involved in a minor controversy when he interviewed comedian and *The Daily Show* host Jon Stewart on *Crossfire.* Stewart was supposed to be there to promote *America (The Rock).* However, instead, he used the opportunity to hit out at *Crossfire* itself, calling the show harmful to political discourse in America and claiming that it had "failed miserably" in terms of political debate and commentary. However, the bulk of his ire was directed towards Carlson in particular. Carlson told Stewart that he should "get a job at journalism school." Stewart replied, "You need to go to one." He later told Carlson that he was "as big a d--- on your show as you are on any show."

Carlson and Begala later stated that Stewart and one of his co-authors, Ben Karlin, had stayed at CNN for over an hour after the show to discuss the points he had made. After his appearance on the show, Stewart said, "It really was not my intention to be disruptive. I truly thought we'd have a goof about how terrible the program is at the top, and move on, but... the combination of their obstinance and my low blood sugar led to *no Bueno.*" However, many years later, in 2021, Stewart tweeted that "I called Tucker Carlson a d--- on national television. It's high time I apologize... to d---s. Never should have lumped you in with that terrible, terrible person."

The Jon Stewart interview was a low point in Carlson's career. On January 5, 2005, a few months after the interview, Jonathan Klein, CNN chief, told Carlson that the network would not be renewing his contract. *Crossfire* was canceled not long after that. In the news release accompanying the announcement, Klein stated that he was looking to change the tone of shows on CNN and elsewhere said that he agreed with much of Stewart's criticisms of *Crossfire.* He "wanted to move CNN away from what he called 'head-butting debate shows.'"

Carlson's version of events was that he had, in fact, already resigned from *Crossfire* way back in April 2004, many months before the Stewart interview, "because I didn't like the partisanship, and I thought in some ways it was kind of a pointless conversation."

Whatever the truth, while Carlson's time at CNN might have ended, his television career was just getting started. In 2003, he had been hired by PBS to head up his own show, *Tucker Carlson: Unfiltered,* which The New Yorker described as being "part of a broader effort to push PBS further to the right ideologically." Despite the Corporation for Public Broadcasting setting aside the funds for another season of *Unfiltered,* Carlson announced that he was leaving the show just a year after it had first aired, saying that he would instead focus on his new MSNBC show, *Tucker.* He also stated that while PBS was among the "least bad" instances of government spending, it was nevertheless still "problematic."

Tucker, which had been originally given the title *The Situation with Tucker Carlson,* made its premiere on MSNBC on June 13, 2005. It also featured Rachel Maddow and Jay Severin as guests on a rotating panel. While the show aired, Carlson also hosted a late-afternoon summary of the 2006 Winter Olympics, and *MSNBC Special Report: Mideast Crisis.* In addition, he was one of several reporters sent to the Virginia Tech campus to report on the aftermath of the Virginia Tech shooting on April 17, 2007. *MSNBC* finally canceled *Tucker* in March 2008 due to low ratings. However, Carlson still stayed with the network as a senior campaign correspondent for the 2008 election. Writing for *The New York Times,* Brian Stelter observed that "during Mr. Carlson's tenure, MSNBC's evening programming moved gradually to the left. His former time slots, 6:00 pm and 9:00 pm, were then occupied by two liberals, Ed Schultz and Rachel Maddow." Carlson's personal take was that the network had changed a lot and "they didn't have a role for me."

As Carlson's profile grew, he took advantage of other media opportunities, such as competing on the reality show, *Dancing with the Stars.* He said he jumped at the opportunity to compete because "I don't do things that I'm not good at very often. I'm psyched to get to do that."

His dance partner on the show was Elena Grinenko, a professional ballroom dance champion, choreographer, and instructor. In preparation for the show, Carlson regularly attended four-hour ballroom dance classes, which clashed with his MSNBC assignment in Lebanon for the *Special Report.* During his two weeks away, Carlson complained about having to miss his classes because "It's hard for me to remember the moves."

Despite his dedication to preparing for the competition, Carlson became the first contestant to be eliminated when the show aired in September 2006.

Carlson had built enough of a name by 2007 to be given a cameo in a season one episode of *30 Rock.* The *Hard Ball* episode received critical praise and was nominated for three awards, winning the Primetime Emmy Award for Outstanding Comedy Series. Carlson also appeared as himself in a season nine episode of *The King of Queens,* in which Doug dreamed about living in an apartment across the hall from Carlson, who offered to talk politics with him any time. He also played himself in the 2008 film *Swing Vote,* a comedy-drama about a presidential election in which one man holds the power to determine the outcome.

Chapter 3

Fox News

In May 2009, Fox News revealed that they had hired Carlson as a Fox News contributor. Subsequently, he featured regularly as a guest panelist on *Red Eye w/Greg Gutfeld,* Fox's late-night satire show, and on the All-Star Panel segment of *Special Report with Bret Baier.* He also served as substitute host of *Hannity* if titular host Sean Hannity could not make a show. And he produced and hosted a special called *Fighting for Our Children's Minds* in September 2010.

The night before then-President Barack Obama's first presidential debate with Mitt Romney in 2012, Carlson took the opportunity to publicize a video recording made back in 2007 of then-Senator Obama being highly critical of the federal government's reaction to Hurricane Katrina and praising his own pastor, Reverend Jeremiah Wright's behavior. Wright's sermons had been a significant cause of controversy during Obama's 2008 presidential campaign.

Many believed that Wright had suggested that America had deserved to be the target of terrorist attacks because of its policies. He summarized the situation as "America's chickens are coming home to roost." Obama had attempted to distance himself from the pastor before cutting ties entirely in 2008, saying, "Our relations with Trinity have been strained by the divisive statements of Reverend Wright, which sharply conflict with our own views."

Carlson's star was on the rise, and in April 2013, Carlson joined Clayton Morris and Alisyn Camerota as a co-host on *Fox & Friends Weekend,* replacing Dave Briggs. However, Carlson really made his mark on the network in November 2016, when he started hosting *Tucker Carlson Tonight*. The first episode replaced *On the Record* and quickly became the network's most-watched show of the year in that time slot, attracting 3.7 million viewers.

Tucker Carlson Tonight remained in the 7 pm slot until January 2017, when it was moved to the 9 pm time slot, replacing Megyn Kelly's show after her departure from the network. That month, *Forbes* reported that *Tucker Carlson Tonight* had "scored consistently high ratings, averaging 2.8 million viewers per night and ranking as the number two cable news program behind *The O'Reilly Factor* in December." The show continued to be popular among viewers, and by March of that year, it was the most-watched cable program in the 9 pm slot. By October, *Tucker Carlson Tonight* was the second-highest rated prime time cable news show after *The Sean Hannity Show* with 3.2 million regular viewers. However, comments by Carlson that immigrants made the country "poorer, dirtier and more divided" saw a number of advertisers boycott the show. However, according to Fox News, the advertisers had not abandoned the network, but had chosen to put their ad spend into other programs.

By early 2019, viewing figures had dropped six percent, causing the show to slip to third most-watched. At least 26 advertisers had stopped investing in the program. There were calls to fire Carlson from the network in March 2019 after some accused him of being sexist and xenophobic following some comments he had made to the radio show *Bubba the Love Sponge.* However, while Carlson might have found himself under fire from the public at large, his viewers still loved him. That week, his show's ratings rose 8%, even with all the boycotts. By the end of the year, Nielsen ratings had

Carlson's show as second only to *The Sean Hannity Show* out of all the cable news shows.

In December 2019, Carlson was the subject of court action when *Playboy* model Karen McDougal sued Fox News for defamation. Carlson had claimed that McDougal had extorted President Donald Trump "out of approximately $150,000 in exchange for her silence about an alleged affair." However, Fox News pushed for a dismissal because "Carlson's statements were not statements of fact and that she failed adequately to allege actual malice." Further, Fox News' lawyers argued that no "reasonable viewer" would ever take Carlson seriously. They calmed that Carlson "cannot be understood to have been stating facts, but instead that he was delivering an opinion using hyperbole for effect" and that Fox News "submits that the use of that word or an accusation of extortion, absent more, is simply 'loose, figurative, or hyperbolic language' that does not give rise to a defamation claim."

Ruling on the case, US District Judge Mary Kay Vyskocil determined that the "'general tenor' of the show should then inform a viewer that he is not 'stating actual facts' about the topics he discusses and is instead engaging in 'exaggeration' and 'non-literal commentary,'" and that given Mr. Carlson's reputation, any reasonable viewer 'arrive[s] with an appropriate amount of skepticism about the statements he makes."

While it was a victory for the network, the verdict was somewhat of a backhanded compliment towards Carlson. Undeterred, Carlson continued to court controversy with comments criticizing the Black Lives Matter movement, causing even more companies to pull their advertising from him, including heavy hitters like T-Mobile, The Walt Disney Company, and Papa John's.

Still, by June 2020. *Tucker Carlson Tonight* hit the number one spot in terms of US cable news shows, attracting an average of four million viewers to push Hannity and Ingraham lower down the scale. By October of the same year, the show was pulling in over five million viewers. 2020 was an exceptional year for the pundit, with his show and *The Sean Hannity Show* closing out the twelve-month period with consistent viewing figures of over four million, the first cable news programs to achieve such figures.

Although Carlson was an open supporter of Donald Trump, he made a point of distancing himself from the former president's post-election legal fights, stating that while the result was "not fair," Trump's legal battle would not overturn the result. In the week following the inauguration of Joe Biden, *Tucker Carlson Tonight* had the unique distinction of the only cable news program not to suffer from a dip in viewership, actually increasing its viewing figures.

Given all this success, it was unsurprising in February 2021 when Carlson announced that he had signed a multiyear deal with Fox News to head up a new weekly podcast alongside a number of monthly specials to be called *Tucker Carlson Originals,* which would be exclusively hosted on the network's sister streaming service, Fox Nation.

Carlson's presentation style and approach to debate have frequently drawn criticism from commentators. He has a mercurial ability to shift between taking the stance of devil's advocate and ethical truth-teller, managing to come across as both laid back and outraged. One of his friends, James Carville, who is also a Democratic strategist and has appeared on Carlson's shows, described the presenter as "one of the world's great contrarians" with a knack for making his opinions appear rebellious even if they are mainstream.

Carlson's producers keep a close focus on his face during remote interviews to capture his reactions. He is known for his scowl, which connects with viewers, encouraging them to share his disapproval of opposite arguments before letting loose with a strong rebuttal.

Carlson has said that he particularly enjoys taking down people he believes think that "I'm a really good person, and you're not."

Carlson uses interruptions as a technique to keep his guests on the back foot, demanding that they answer his questions or focusing on something the guest has said in the past. Writing for *Politico,* Jack Shafer has said that "When the host barks questions in your earpiece, you can't help but jolt to life like a puppet on a string," arguing that for a guest to be successful on Carlson's show, they need to have his same level of quick thinking and ability to stay calm under pressure.

Chapter 4

The Daily Caller

Carlson teamed up with Neil Patel, a former college roommate (and former aide to Dick Cheney), to put together a political news website called *The Daily Caller.* The site launched on January 11, 2010, with Carlson acting as editor-in-chief and occasionally contributing opinion pieces with Patel. Funded by conservative activist Foster Freiis, the site was so successful that just a month later, *The Daily Caller* was included in the White House rotating press pool.

Despite his strong conservative leanings, Carlson stated that *The Daily Caller* would be "breaking stories of importance" rather than being tied to any particular ideology, explicitly stating that "We're not enforcing any kind of ideological orthodoxy on anyone." However, despite these lofty ideals, Mickey Kaus, one of the site's columnists, quit after Carlson squashed a piece he had written criticizing Fox News' coverage of the immigration policy debate. Given Carlson's contractual links to Fox News, it would not have been possible for him to run such an article, but the action certainly ran contra to the site's alleged philosophy.

In June 2010, *The Daily Caller* ran a feature on several emails that the site had obtained from members of JournoList. JournoList was an invite-only liberal forum whose members were "several hundred journalists, academics and policy experts." The founder of the forum, Ezra Klein, was a journalist, political analyst, columnist for *New York Times, and* podcaster. He had a policy of excluding media reporters and conservatives from the forum. When Carlson attempted to join the forum in May 2010, Klein turned down his application. Instead, Klein offered to set up a bipartisan forum with Carlson, but Carlson turned down the opportunity. Instead, *Daily Caller* employers pretended to be an editor of the *Arkansas Times* in order to access JournoList. The emails they were able to gather as a result allegedly outlined an attempt to formulate the most effective talking points in order to defeat Palin and McCain and help elect Obama president." Carlson summed up the emails, writing, "Again and again, we discovered members of JournoList working to coordinate talking points on behalf of Democratic politicians, principally Barack Obama. That is not journalism, and those who engage in it are not journalists. They should stop pretending to be. The news organizations they work for should stop pretending, too... I've been in journalism my entire adult life, and have often defended it against fellow conservatives who claim the news business is fundamentally corrupt. It's harder to make that defense now. It will be easier when honest (and, yes, liberal) journalists denounce what happened on JournoList as wrong."

In addition, *The Daily Caller* uncovered remarks made by Dave Weigel of *The Washington Post* "wishing for the death of Rush Limbaugh" alongside other distasteful comments, rendering his position at the publication "untenable" and forcing his resignation. Not long after, Klein permanently shut down JournoList.

In February 2012, *The Daily Caller* published a series of articles co-written by Carlson that were meant to be an exposé of Media Matters for America and its founder, David Brock, a liberal watchdog organization that monitored and critiqued conservative media outlets. Ironically, while there were those who agreed that Media Matters was far from perfect in its approach, in the words of Jack Shafer, "*Daily Caller* is attacking Media Matters with bad journalism and lame propaganda." Further, Shafter, a Reuters media critic, said that *The Daily Caller* had presented little more than conjecture with no hard evidence, relying on "anonymously sourced crap."

As his broadcasting duties demanded more of his time, Carlson took more of a back seat role at *The Daily Caller*, and in June 2020, Carlson sold his share in the site to Patel. Carlson revealed his motives for selling his interest by revealing that "I haven't had editorial input" since the prime-time show began. Neil runs it. I wasn't adding anything. So we made it official."

Carlson has also written a number of books over the years, starting with his memoir, *Politicians, Partisans and Parasites: My Adventures in Cable News* which was published in September 2003 by Warner Books. The memoir focused on his television news experiences and received positive reviews, including ones from the *Washingtonian* and *Publishers Weekly,* which singled out Carlson's sense of humor for special praise.

In May 2017, Carlson signed an impressive eight-figure, two-book deal with Threshold Editions, the conservative imprint of Big Five publisher Simon & Schuster. His first book under the deal shot straight to number one on the *New York Times* bestseller list. *Ship of Fools: How a Selfish Ruling Class Is Bringing America to the Brink of Revolution* was a non-fiction political book that argued that typical Americans were being failed by a so-called "ruling class." Carlson used the notion of a US ship of state to explore the notion that the current political and economic elite were incompetent and had no concept of what their citizens needed from them yet refused to accept any criticism. In the book, he attacked politicians of both political parties, as well as modern entrepreneurs, whom he felt had contributed to the widening gap between rich and poor, an act of betrayal against those liberal values they espoused. Carlson excluded Trump as one of these supposed 'fools,' arguing that his election was an aberration and an attempt by the populace to send a message to those steering the ship.

Carlson is a self-confessed 'Deadhead' (fan of the Grateful Dead, a successful rock band) and once said that he had been to more than fifty of their concerts. As such, he revealed that the title of his book, *Ship of Fools,* was a tribute to the Grateful Dead's song of the same name.

Ship of Fools will be followed up by his second book, which is due for release in August 2021. *The Long Slide: Thirty Years in American Journalism* will contain "a few of [Carlson's] favorite pieces—annotated with new commentary and insight—to memorialize the tolerance and diversity of thought that the media used to celebrate instead of punish." In addition, the text will also target Threshold Editions themselves to examine the controversy surrounding their decision not to publish Missouri Senator Josh Hawley's *The Tyranny of Big Tech.*

Chapter 5

Abortion and Death Penalty

Carlson is regularly described in the media as a conservative or paleoconservative. In a piece for *Intelligencer,* Park MacDougald called Carlson a "middle American radical," a term he defined as one who holds populist economic opinions, is against corporatocracy, hold strongly defined ideas surrounding immigration, nationalism, and race, and likes strong US presidents. MacDougald claimed that these principles were at the ideological heart of Trumpism – and Carlson has always been a vocal supporter of Trump while being unafraid to criticize him.

Carlson is a devout Episcopalian and has said that he "loves the liturgy, [but] abhors the liberals who run the denomination." As such, he is firmly opposed to abortion, describing it as the only non-negotiable political issue.

In a segment on *Tucker Carlson Tonight,* Carlson singled out then-presidential candidate, musician Kanye West for expressing pro-life opinions, expressing admiration for his outspokenness, since Republicans were "too afraid" to come out like this. When West launched a campaign in South Carolina, he talked about how his father wanted to abort him, as well as going into his feelings about his then-wife Kim Kardashian having their first child, "even when I didn't want to."

Carlson described West as "the most compelling voice against abortion and Planned Parenthood," going on to say that "The most widely heard Christian evangelist in America is not ordained. Instead, he is a rapper married to a Kardashian who, by the way, everyone says is crazy… Kanye West is running for president, but that's not really the headline. The headline is that on core conservative issues, not political issues like legislation before Congress, but on foundational questions about life and children and what happens when you die, no one with a national platform has been more honest or sincere or effective than Kanye West has been, maybe in generations. It's all pretty shocking, really. Talk about an unlikely messenger. But it's real..."

As well as being pro-life, Carlson is against capital punishment, believing that it "deserves more vigorous debate." In 2003, he told *Salon* that I'm opposed to the death penalty as I am adamantly opposed to abortion."

However, in 2010, Carlson made headlines when, despite his beliefs, he said that he felt that Michael Vick, Philadelphia Eagles quarterback, should be executed for his involvement in a dogfighting ring. The football star instead spent 21 months in federal prison.

A few days later, speaking on Sean Hannity's show, Carlson said, "Anybody who looks into how he mistreated these dogs and personally tortured them to death gets upset, and I overspoke. I'm not comfortable with the death penalty under any circumstances. Of course I don't think he should be executed." He added that child molesters weren't given second chances, and the President had been wrong to praise Vick, since "I do think what he did is truly appalling.

Chapter 6

Politics, Economics, Environment

Carlson is a confirmed Republican, although he was registered as a Democrat in Washington DC for fourteen years from 2006-20. Carlson has said that he registered as a Democrat so he could have the right to vote in primaries for mayoral elections in the district, which he described as "a one-party state." He had a policy of always voting for "the more corrupt candidate over the idealist" in order to combat progressivism. Despite being registered as a Democrat, Carlson campaigned for Republicans and associated causes.

Carlson voted for George W Bush in the 2000 election but became disillusioned with the then-president due to his response to the 9/11 terrorist attacks. Carlson felt that Bush should have immediately returned to Washington, DC, where he and his "wife and children stayed inside [their] house ... unprotected a few miles from the scene of a terrorist attack." By the time of the 2004 election, Carlson had concluded that "by my criteria, Bush isn't much of a conservative." He also had issues with the government's approach to the Iraq War and the direction the Republican Party was taking. As a result, he decided not to vote.

Carlson was not particularly impressed with the Republican nominee for the 2012 election either. Mitt Romney had backed healthcare reforms while governor of Massachusetts that Carlson disagreed with. He said, "out of 315 million Americans, the Republican Party managed to find the one guy who couldn't run on Obamacare."

However, Carlson's attitude towards Republican candidates changed with the advent of Trump. Carlson is a strong advocate for personal responsibility and has stated that "I hate all nanny-state regulations, such as seat belt laws and smoking bans." As such, Trump had a definite appeal for the television pundit.

During the former reality star's presidency, *Politico* described Carlson as perhaps the highest-profile proponent of 'Trumpism' — a blend of anti-immigrant nationalism, economic populism, and America First isolationism." While Carlson did not always support everything that Trump did, he was far more scathing towards Trump's critics, leading some commentators to dub Carlson the epitome of "anti-anti-Trump" ideas.

Despite this support for Trump, Carlson allegedly told people that he had voted for independent candidate Kanye West in the 2020 election. However, it was unclear whether Carlson was being genuine or "merely joking."

Carlson is known for doubting the impact of climate change and often hosts guests who go against the general scientific consensus on the subject. For example, in one segment on *Tucker Carlson Tonight,* he accused Democratic leaders of leveraging climate change in a bid to win votes rather than having any genuine concern for the environment or scientific truth. Following a series of wildfires, Carlson argued that there was nothing to link climate change to the severity of the fires.

"Climate change, they said, caused these fires. They didn't explain how exactly that happened. How did climate change do that?" he asked. "In the hands of Democratic politicians, climate change is like systemic racism in the sky. You can't see it, but rest assured it's everywhere, and it's deadly." He went on to add, "And like systemic racism, it is your fault," Carlson continued. "The American middle class did it. They caused climate change. They ate too many hamburgers. They drove too many SUVs. They had too many children."

In fact, fire experts stated that changing global temperatures and weather patterns had combined to create ideal conditions for a longer, more aggressive fire season in 2020.

Carlson's comments came a year after he had described the student environmental protest Climate Strike a "coordinated left-wing political protest." He likened the modern climate change movement to Mao's Great Leap Forward, commenting, "And there you have the modern left's climate agenda: no drinking straws, no automobiles, no airplanes, no meat, no democracy."

Early in his career, Carlson was an advocate for libertarian economics. He had supported Ron Paul's presidential candidacy in 1988 and 2008 when Paul ran as a Libertarian and Republican, respectively. However, since 2018, he has been vocal in his opposition to libertarianism, taking a more populist economic approach. He has stated that "market capitalism is not a religion." He has also stated that too fast economic and technological change can lead to social and political upheaval, pointing to President Roosevelt's intervention in the early 1900s for potentially heading off a communist revolution.

Carlson has also criticized hedge funds and private equity. He has described the business model of capital firms as being "Take over an existing company for a short period of time, cut costs by firing employees, run up the debt, extract the wealth and move on, sometimes leaving retirees without their earned pensions... Meanwhile, a remarkable number of the companies are now bankrupt or extinct."

Chapter 7

The 2020 Election

In September 2020, in the run-up to the presidential election, Carlson told his viewers that the reason why the Democrats had been pushing mail-in voting was to build "uncertainty over the outcome of the election so they can manipulate the results." Following Joe Biden's victory, Carlson alleged that there had been instances of electoral fraud. On *Tucker Carlson Tonight,* he recited names of allegedly deceased individuals who had returned from the grave to vote in Georgia. However, investigative journalists researching his claims discovered that some of the people he had claimed had been dead were very much alive and more than capable of voting.

However, while Carlson had backed the notion of electoral fraud, he was more skeptical of claims made by former federal prosecutor Sidney Powell, who had stated that Venezuela, Cuba, and other unnamed communist interests had hacked into voting machines in order to sway the result. Carlson conceded that "what Powell was describing would amount to the single greatest crime in American history," but went on to say that when he had approached her for evidence of her allegations, she became "angry and told us to stop contacting her." Trump defenders attacked Carlson for his stance, despite the fact that Powell was soon dropped from Trump's legal team.

The months following Trump's defeat saw a great deal of civil unrest, including the storming of the US Capitol on January 6, 2001. In February 2021, attorney general nominee Merrick Garland pledged at his confirmation hearing to oversee the prosecution of "white supremacists and others" who had been involved in the violent protest. Carlson protested that "There's no evidence that white supremacists were responsible for what happened on January 6. That's a lie," a claim that was rated as false by Politifact. Several protestors had proven links to white supremacist groups, and many supremacist symbols had been displayed by protestors.

Carlson's remarks led Philip Bump of *The Washington Post* to note that Carlson was drawing little to no distinction between the notions of "being involved" and "being responsible for" in a bid to "undercut the public understanding of what happened and, by extension, to soften the implications for Trump and his supporters."

In June 2021, Carlson proposed the idea that the Capitol storming had, in fact, been a false flag FBI operation mounted to "suppress political dissent." He claimed that government documents revealed that FBI operatives were organizing the attack on the Capitol on January 6," and pointed to the mention of key unindicted co-conspirators in prosecutors' court filings, meaning that in "potentially every single case, they were FBI operatives."

Legal experts countered this by pointing out that prosecutors cannot describe an undercover agent as an unindicted co-conspirator. Further, one of these unindicted co-conspirators was soon identified as Stewart Rhodes, founder and leader of Oath Keepers, a known far-right anti-government militia; another was most likely to be the wife of one of the named conspirators.

Darren Beattie of Revolver News had written pieces that had inspired the segment, and Carlson had him as a guest on his show.

Beattie's presence was problematic since he had been fired as a Trump speechwriter in 2018 after CNN questioned the White House about why he had been present at a gathering of white nationalists. His history meant that his opinions had a clear bias and possible agenda.

Carlson had also said that Russian president Vladimir Putin had been asking "fair questions" when he drew comparisons between the shooting of a rioter inside the Capitol to the poisoning of Alexei Navalny, a Russian opposition leader, lawyer, and anti-corruption activist, a poisoning Putin denied having anything to do with.

Matt Gaetz and Marjorie Taylor Greene, Republican House members, were quick to jump onto Carlson's story, while Republican congressman Paul Gosar entered the Revolver News article into the *Congressional Record* during a House Oversight Committee hearing since it contained information concerning the "infiltration and incitement of the January 6 protest by federal officials".

Chapter 8

Foreign Policy and Immigration

Carlson has a long history of being critical of foreign intervention, believing that "the US ought to hesitate before intervening abroad."

Carlson was originally a supporter of the Iraq War, but a year after the invasion of Iraq, he became a more vocal opponent of the war. He told *The New York Observer,* "I think it's a total nightmare and disaster, and I'm ashamed that I went against my own instincts in supporting it."

Carlson had similar feelings about Iran and, in July 2017, stated that "we actually don't face any domestic threat from Iran." He asked Max Boot, a Russian-American author, consultant, editorialist, lecturer, and military historian, to "tell me how many Americans in the United States have been murdered by terrorists backed by Iran since 9/11?"

More controversially, Carlson made a number of comments during call-in segments on the radio show *Bubba the Love Sponge* between 2006-09. He argued that Iraq was not worth the effort of invading because it was a nation filled with "semi-literate primitive monkeys" who "don't use toilet paper or forks." In addition, he had strong words for "lunatic Muslims who are behaving like animals," arguing that anyone who stood for president on a ticket aimed at killing "as many of them as [they] can" would easily win. These segments resurfaced in 2019 when they were released online by Media Matters for America, resulting in a backlash against Carlson, with some advertisers pulling their support for his show.

Carlson has often been credited with influencing Trump's policies, and *The New York Times* ran a piece that claimed that Carlson had played an important part in preventing Trump from launching military strikes against Iran after an American drone was shot down in June 2019. Allegedly, Carlson said to Trump that if he followed his advisors in ordering the strikes, he would guarantee a loss at the next election.

He has also pointed out that "if we're still in Afghanistan, 19 years, sad years, later, what makes us think there's a quick way out of Iran?"

Carlson was in agreement with Trump's plans for a border wall between the United States and Mexico, arguing that it was essential to "restore sovereignty" between the two nations. In fact, in an interview in July 2018, Carlson argued that Mexico had had a far greater impact on US elections than Russia ever had simply by influencing elections through the medium of mass immigration. He felt that mass immigration had made the US "dirtier," "poorer," and "more divided," adding that it had "badly hurt this country's natural landscape. Taking Hazleton, Pennsylvania as an example, where the Hispanic population had grown rapidly to become a majority, Carlson called this "more change than human beings are designed to digest."

Journalist Philip Bump countered this by pointing out that the number of Mexicans living in the US had, in fact, declined since 2009, questioning, What good has it done Mexico to have a number of its citizens move to the United States and gain the right to vote?"

Nevertheless, Carlson also backed Trump's move to impose tariffs on Mexico unless Mexico did more to prevent illegal immigration to the US. He argued that "When the United States is attacked by a hostile foreign power, it must strike back. And make no mistake, Mexico is a hostile foreign power."

In May 2019, Carlson stated that "The flood of illegal workers into the United States has damaged our communities, ruined our schools, burdened our healthcare system and fractured our national unity." Later that same year, he alleged that immigrants had been responsible for making the Potomac River "dirtier and dirtier."

Echoing his earlier remarks, in April 2021, Carlson claimed that the Democratic Party "is trying to replace the current electorate, the voters now casting ballots, with new people, more obedient voters from the Third World," going on to say, "Everyone wants to make a racial issue out of it, 'Ooh, the white replacement theory.' No, no, no, this is a voting rights question. I have less political power because they are importing a brand-new electorate. Why should I sit back and take that?"

Carlson's comments caused significant controversy, with the Anti-Defamation League (ADL), among others, arguing that Carlson was clearly supporting the so-called Great Replacement. This white nationalist conspiracy theory holds that white people are being deliberately and systematically replaced through the medium of declining white birth rates combined with high levels of immigration. Jonathan Greenblatt, ADL CEO, wrote an open letter to Fox News demanding that Carlson be fired, calling his arguments not just a dog whistle to racists — [but] a bullhorn.

Lachlan Murdoch, Fox Corporation CEO, backed Carlson, countering that Carlson had made it clear that he was rejecting replacement theory by saying he was discussing a voting rights question. Greenblatt was not swayed, claiming that this had made things "worse, because he's using a straw man – voting rights – to give an underhanded endorsement of white supremacist beliefs while ironically suggesting it's not really white supremacism."

Conversely, Carlson has opined that Russia is not a significant threat to the United States and has called for the two powers to work together in situations such as the Syrian Civil War, where they should combine forces against common foes such as the Islamic State of Iraq and the Levant (ISIS).

Carlson's stance has led journalists such as Peter Beinart of *The Atlantic* to call Carlson an "apologist" for Trump on Russian matters. Countering the accusation, Carlson dismissed allegations that Donald Trump Jr. had been happy to receive anti-Clinton information from a Russian government official as taking things to a "new level of hysteria" and Trump Jr. had merely been "gossiping with foreigners."

However, in May 2019, Robert Mueller released a statement to say that the Special Counsel Investigation on Russian interference in the 2016 election had not cleared President Trump of obstruction of justice. In response, Carlson described Mueller as being "sleazy and dishonest."

In December 2019, Carlson pointed out that the irony, of course, is that Putin, for all his faults, does not hate America as much as many of these [liberals] do… They really dislike our country. And they call other people traitors because they're mouthing the talking points of Putin."

In line with his opinion that America should not interfere with other country's politics, Carlson opposed the removal of Syrian President Bashar al-Assad and has glossed over accusations of human rights violations by the Assad regime in the Syrian Civil War. He has also queried whether Assad was indeed behind the Douma chemical attack that killed dozens of people. He linked it with a similar attack that had been carried out the previous year and suggested that they were false flag attacks set up to cast aspersions on the Assad government.

When President Trump made history by meeting with the North Korean leader Kim Jong-un, during an appearance on *Fox & Friends,* Carlson said, "there's no defending the North Korean regime, it's the last real Stalinist regime in the world. It's a disgusting place obviously [but] you've got to be honest about what it means to lead a country, it means killing people… [While] not on the scale that the North Koreans do… a lot of countries commit atrocities, including a number that [the United States] are closely allied with."

While Carlson has demonstrated opposition to American interference in other countries, he is also vehement about his opinions on immigration, both legal and illegal. He often states that Democrats use migration as a means to increase their voter base.

In a piece for *Politico* written in January 2016, Carlson spoke about his agreement with Trump's policies on immigration, such as his promised "Muslim ban," and he called for other Republican candidates to be more active in making immigration a significant part of their policies.

Carlson's stance on migration has led to some accusing him of promoting racism. Heidi Beirich of the Southern Poverty Law Center once stated that "Carlson probably has been the No. 1 commentator mainstreaming bedrock principles of white nationalism in [the US]," an accusation Carlson vehemently denies saying, "I'm not a racist. I hate racism."

In fact, Carlson has accused liberals of being the true racists. Appearing with Alex Jones in 2015, Carlson spoke about the Obama administration, saying, "They categorize people by race in a way that, you know, you cannot even imagine. Thirty years ago, you would have said, 'Wait a second, that's like Nazi stuff.'"

In August 2018, Carlson claimed that the South African government was deliberately targeting white farmers purely because "they are the wrong skin color," falsely accusing the country's president of changing the constitution to enable land thefts from white farmers. A number of publications, including *The New York Times* and *The Wall Street Journal,* denounced the segment as being false or misleading because violence against white farmers was, in fact, at its lowest level ever. Further, the reforms under question had yet to come into effect and were mainly aimed at disused land.

Perhaps demonstrating Carlson's influence on then-President Trump, the President tweeted to state that he had told Secretary of State Mike Pompeo to "closely study the South Africa land and farm seizure and large scale killing of farmers." The South African government called Trump's tweet "misinformed" and said that it would use diplomatic channels to deal with the issue.

The following evening after the controversial segment, Carlson recognized that the proposed amendment had not passed into law yet and revealed that no farms had yet been seized, but he stopped short of conceding that he'd made any mistakes.

In July 2019, Carlson ended an episode of *Tucker Carlson Tonight* with a diatribe aimed at

Representative Ilhan Omar (D-MN), who had been granted asylum, saying that she was ungrateful to her new home nation and was "living proof that the way we practice immigration has become dangerous to this country." *The Guardian* described the segment as being "racially loaded" and filled with "anti-immigrant rhetoric."

Congresswoman Omar herself replied on Twitter, writing that "advertisers should not be underwriting this kind of dangerous, hateful rhetoric."

A few days later, *The Daily Beast* ran an opinion piece on the incident, pointing out that due to "right-wing attacks that have then been amplified by members of Congress and the president," Omar had been subject to a number of death threats since being elected, and pointed out that Carlson's repeated criticism had contributed to this situation.

Undeterred, following the August 2019 El Paso shooting, Carlson stated that he believed that white supremacy was a "hoax" and "conspiracy theory used to divide the country and keep a hold on power." The shooting had been carried out by Patrick Wood Crusius, a 21-year-old from

Allen, Texas, who had released an anti-immigration manifesto aimed at countering the so-called "Hispanic invasion." Carlson posed this rhetorical question: If you were to take "the combined membership of every white supremacist group in America – would they be able to fit inside a college football stadium?" *The Washington Post* pointed to a spate of other attacks, writing, "Carlson's argument is belied by many experts and seemingly contradicted by a recent wave of deadly attacks by men motivated by those views."

Most recently, and perhaps most controversially, Carlson questioned the motives of the Black Lives Matter protestors following the death of George Floyd. Floyd was arrested after a store clerk suspected him of using a counterfeit $20 bill. Four police officers quickly arrived at the scene, where one officer restrained Floyd by kneeling on his neck and back for almost ten minutes, killing him.

Floyd's death resulted in a wave of anti-racism protests around the world, but Carlson claimed that these protests were "definitely not about black lives, and remember that when they come for you, and at this rate, they will."

While Fox News claimed that Carlson had been talking about Democratic leaders rather than the protestors, many advertisers pulled their ads from *Tucker Carlson Tonight.* Carlson continued to criticize Black Lives Matter, stating that the continued protests were more about ideological domination rather than any genuine concern over police brutality.

The police officers were charged with murder, but Carlson stated in 2021 that "there was no physical evidence that George Floyd was murdered by a cop" and "the autopsy showed that George Floyd almost certainly died of a drug overdose." This, despite two autopsies showing that Floyd had died as a result of ex-police officer Derek Chauvin kneeling on his neck for a prolonged period. While Floyd did have drugs in his system at the time of his death, the autopsies found that these were not the cause of his death.

When Chauvin was found guilty of murder, Carlson went on record to say that he believed that the jury had been threatened into the verdict because of Black Lives Matter protests rather than because of any serious consideration of witness testimony or video evidence of the event. He called these protests "nearly a year of burning and looting and murder by BLM."

Chapter 9

COVID-19

When COVID-19 first hit the news in early 2020, Carlson used his show to warn people about the virus. On March 9, 2020, Carlson began his show with a statement: "People you trust, people you probably voted for, have spent weeks minimizing what is clearly a very serious problem... But they're wrong. It's definitely not just the flu." It is said that he influenced then-President Trump to take the virus more seriously. Carlson later revealed to *Vanity Fair* that he had indeed spoken to the president and encouraged him to take the outbreak more seriously.

However, by spring of 2020, Carlson began to change his stance, questioning the seriousness of the virus, opposing social distancing, as well as the use of masks and vaccines. He spoke out against stay-at-home orders and mocked Anthony Fauci, NIAID director. He backed rural protests against lockdowns: "The threat to rural America from this virus is minuscule, so why are we punishing the people who live outside the cities?"

In 2021, Carlson ran a number of segments querying the safety of COVID-19 vaccines, suggesting that US officials were "lying" about them. He wondered why the CDC advised the fully vaccinated to persevere with mask-wearing and distancing, opining, "maybe [the vaccine] doesn't work, and they're simply not telling you that... what's the other potential explanation? We can't think of one."

Fauci denounced Carlson's remarks as a "crazy conspiracy theory, but while Carlson stated that he "never for a minute doubted the effectiveness of the vaccines, you still have to wonder why the people in charge are acting like it doesn't work."

Carlson went on to refer to the VAERS database in subsequent segments, arguing that it showed that over the past five months, roughly 30 people per day had died after receiving a COVID-19 vaccine. However, *Politifact* described this claim as misleading because the VAERS database can be misused and does not demonstrate an established causal link between vaccines and any resultant deaths.

Carlson persisted in his criticism of official reactions to the COVID-19 virus, calling those who wore masks outdoors "zealots and neurotics" and likened making children wear masks to child abuse. He stated that "Your response when you see children wearing masks as they play should be no different from your response to seeing someone beat a kid in Walmart... Call the police immediately, contact child protective services. Keep calling until someone arrives."

Chapter 10

The Future

Despite all the controversy and questionable interview techniques, there is no doubt that Carlson is currently riding high and enjoys immense popularity among viewers. In fact, so broad is his appeal that there are rumors that he will use his platform as a springboard to run for President in the 2024 election.

It is not so strange an idea. As Luke Thompson, Republican strategist puts it, "He's a talented communicator with a massive platform. I think if he runs he'd be formidable."

While Carlson has always been a Trump supporter, and general opinion at the moment is that Trump will launch another campaign in the 2024 election, Carlson would be a natural successor since he is a prominent figurehead of "Trumpism." He also shares Trump's television experience, since not only is *Tucker Carlson Tonight* the highest-rated cable news program in history, segments from his show broadcast on the Fox News YouTube channel have garnered over 60 million views and number among the network's most popular videos.

Politico ran a piece on the rumor and interviewed sixteen prominent Republicans. They found a consensus that if Carlson decided to run, he would be a formidable contender. Sam Nunberg, a former aide to Trump who also knows Carlson, said, "Let me put it this way: If Biden wins and Tucker decided to run, he'd be the nominee." However, he doubted that Carlson ever would stand because he's so disgusted with politicians." Other friends also express doubt that he would be interested in leaving his prime-time TV show for a career in politics.

Neither Carlson nor Fox News would comment on the idea for the *Politico* piece, so at the time of writing, the idea is pure speculation.

One thing is sure: Regardless of one's opinion of Carlson and his views, he is unlikely to be going away any time soon.

Made in United States
Troutdale, OR
08/05/2023

11837463R00040